Web of October

Rereading Martin Carter

RUPERT ROOPNARAINE

Peepal Tree Press

First published in 1988
Peepal Tree Press
53, Grove Farm Crescent
Leeds LS16 6BZ
Yorkshire
England

©Rupert Roopnaraine 1986

No part of this publication may be
reproduced or transmitted in any form
or by any means without permission.

ISBN 0 948833 18 1

to the generation of 1953, in another October
for Martin, right popular philosopher
and for Eusi Kwayana, my teacher

... for whatsoever the philosopher saith should be done, he (the poet) giveth a perfect picture of it in some one by whom he presupposeth it was done, so as he coupleth the general notion with the particular example. A perfect picture, I say, for he yieldeth to the powers of the mind an image of that whereof the philosopher bestoweth but a wordish description, which doth neither strike, pierce, nor possess the sight of the soul so much as that other doth... for conclusion, I say the philosopher teacheth but he teacheth obscurely; that is to say, he teacheth them that are already taught. But the poet is the food for the tenderest stomachs; the poet is indeed the right popular philosopher.

— Philip Sidney

CONTENTS

Rereading Martin Carter   7

POEMS OF OCTOBER

Requiem for Louis La Roche	31
Your October Words	33
June and October	34
Images of October	36
Light Steps	38
October Pleasantry	41
Of Music in October	43
Words of Shame	46
Take These The Gift: Poem for Eusi	48
Ode for Samora Machel	50
Return to Reason	52
Song at Point of Path	60
In Memoriam Augusta Mendonca Read	64

Rereading Martin Carter

YOU ARE INVOLVED

This I have learnt:
to-day a speck
to-morrow a hero
hero or monster
you are consumed!

Like a jig
shakes the loom.
Like a web
Is spun the pattern
all are involved!
all are consumed!

This short poem is one of the best known and most quoted of Martin Carter's poems. It is the final poem of his best known collection, *Poems of Resistance*, published in 1954. This little book of eighteen poems was an inspiring cultural expression of the Guyanese people's fight against colonial rule. Branded 'subversive literature,' it was seized in a police raid during the repression which followed the landing of British troops and the suspension of the constitution in October 1953.

Why does this particular poem end the book?

To answer this question, we have to understand how the poem works and what it means. The title of the poem is

'You Are Involved' and it is usually taken to be a poem about involvement, more, a poem urging commitment and involvement, usually in a struggle for justice.

But there is much more to this little poem, as there is much more than a call to arms in *Poems of Resistance*, although there is that primarily.

Indeed, 'You Are Involved' can be said to be pointing in the direction of that aspect of Martin Carter's poetry — some call it private or non-political — which did not escape the notice of his best readers.[1] This area of his concerns as a poet has become more and more insistent in the dense and difficult poems of recent years. 'Proem,' written in 1974, provides an illustration.

PROEM

Not, in the saying of you, are you
said. Baffled and like a root
stopped by a stone you turn back questioning
the tree you feed. But what the leaves hear
is not what the roots ask. Inexhaustibly,
being at one time what was to be said
and at another time what has been said
the saying of you remains the living of you
never to be said. But, enduring
you change with the change that changes
and yet are not of the changing of any of you.
Ever yourself, you are always about
to be yourself in something else ever with me.

---

1. See for example, Wilson Harris, 'The Place of the Poet in Modern Society: A Glance at Two Guyanese Poets,' in *Explorations*, ed. Hena Maes-Jelinek, (Dangaroo Press, Denmark, 1981); William Carr, 'Introduction' to *Poems of Affinity* (Release Publishers, Georgetown, Guyana, 1980).

It is not necessary to argue that this little known and less quoted of Martin Carter's poems which opens the 1977 collection, *Poems of Succession*, is involuted, dense and complex. By comparison, 'You Are Involved' is a model of austerity and simplicity. But the preoccupations of 'Proem' – and they are the preoccupations with the coming into being and activity of poetry itself – are not new. They were always there, less obsessively and more tentatively, but they flicker from time to time through the youthful songs of protest of the anti- colonial revolution. They are the preoccupations that are inscribed at the heart of 'You Are Involved'.

The title of our poem, 'You Are Involved', has some unusual features, and it is with these that we must begin.

It is not a line lifted from the body of the poem itself, but it is, in its construction, exactly like lines 5, 10 and 11, the closing lines of the two stanzas. Consisting *only* of words that occur in these three lines, the title is locked into the poem and implicated in the pattern of its motions and therefore in the logic of its meaning. This emerges only as the poem unfolds, as its repetitions, or echoes, begin to register.

It is reasonable to say that the poem invites us to treat its title as part of a whole. Indeed, it is only when the title is treated as the first line of a poem of twelve lines that the balance of its stanzas is asserted and their symmetry revealed: six:six instead of five:six.

We can see how the title participates in the central pattern of the whole:

        YOU ARE INVOLVED
        ....
        ....
        ....
        ....
        you are consumed!

>   ....
>   ....
>   ....
>   ....
>   all are involved!
>   all are consumed!

But because it is the title, of course, it is not in the same register as the poem proper, even though it seems to be at one with its tone and feeling. While outside the poem proper, it may be either where the poem began, the line that first im-pressed itself on the poet and forced itself out through him; or, it may be what came after the fact, outside of the poetic experience altogether and after its embodiment in language, but what sums it up: either a point of departure or a point of arrival.

At the beginning of his analysis of Keats' 'Ode to a Grecian Urn,' Leo Spitzer writes that he feels justified in beginning as he does by 'the title of the poem, "Ode to a Grecian Urn," which though located outside of the poem proper still belongs to it and contains the orientation intended for us by the poet, who, as is always the case, *speaks in his title to his public as a critic*' (my emphasis).[2]

In the case of our title, it also has this difference: whereas the poem proper consists of what is spoken by a narrator created by the poet for this purpose, the title comes from the poet himself, speaking in his own voice, unmediated by the narrative *persona*. After all, according to what turns out to be the logic of the poem itself, only the poet can be capable of utterance after the final line of the poem since the narrator, having dissolved into the all who are consumed, has been to all intents and purposes snuffed out. That he speaks to his public 'as a critic' is the *sign* that

---

2. Leo Spitzer, *Essays on English and American Literature* (Princeton University Press, Princeton, NJ, 1968) p. 72

marks the poet's triumph over the experience which is of death and dying: he has extricated himself symbolically through the creation of the poem and, within it, of a proxy who speaks 'from the other side': the 'I' of line 1.

Let us next note that the 'you' that greets us right here at the outset is a word of great complexity and range of function. First of all, the 'you' is a duality: it contains a double reference — it is used to address both a single person and many persons, that is, it is both singular and plural. Important implications flow from this simple fact. In his brilliant 'philological' analysis of an American advertisement, Leo Spitzer has demonstrated how this very ambiguity of the 'you' was exploited in the strategies of the advertisement.[3] (The verbal text of the advertisement under scrutiny — it also has a visual text — is the famous one promoting a particular brand of orange juice: 'From the sunkist groves of California/ Fresh for you'.) Drawing on the philosophy of grammar to uncover the nature of the 'you,' Spitzer writes:

> 'You' is a startling word: it calls up the dormant ego in every human being: 'you' is in fact nothing but the ego seen by another; it also suggests someone outside of us who is able to say 'you' and who feels akin to 'us' as a fellow man.[4]

Perhaps its most notorious example, footnoted by Spitzer, is its use in the wartime enlistment poster by James Montgomery Flagg: 'Uncle Sam needs YOU for the United States Army'. This cartoon, more so than any other example, effectively exploits 'this personal susceptibility of the individual to any address which is intended generally.' The English 'you' can do this, Spitzer argues, because it:

---

3. *Ibid.*, p.251
4. *Ibid.*, p.271

> ...enjoys an ambiguity to a degree unknown in the main European languages, which are characterised by greater inflection; it is equally applicable to a singular or a plural audience, and in advertising, this double reference is fully exploited: the advertiser, while preparing his copy for the general public, thinks the 'you' as an 'all of you' — but intends it to be interpreted as a 'you personally,' applicable to individual A, B, or C, ... *Though he is only one of millions, every single individual is individually addressed and flattered.* (my emphasis)

The 'you' of our title works in a somewhat similar way. That is, it has the effect of actively drawing the individual reader into a wider community of persons, or, as the poem will demonstrate, into a wider community of victims.

Our first word singles out an individual from all of humanity (the reader) who then proceeds in the company of the narrator to merge his individual being into humanity as a whole. In our own case, though he is only one of millions, every single individual is individually addressed and implicated. The title beckons to the reader to approach, step in and live out the poem's experience of annihilation.

Now while it is true that the 'you' is ambivalent and is applicable to a singular and plural audience, that is, to one or to all, it is as a singular that it first presents itself and makes its appeal.

Unlike in the case of Spitzer's advertisement, our 'you' is the first, not the last word. This is why our 'you' contains its plural reference *only as a potentiality* when it first hails us. It is not until after we have accepted the invitation and entered into the poem proper and travelled down to the final 'all' of the last line that one of the important motions of the poem is revealed, or better, is activated: the plural 'all' reaches back to the singular 'you' of the title and triggers its plural content. This is to say that the 'you' which began only as an address to a single individual has acquired through the process of our experience of the whole poem, a plural audience: all of humanity. There is a suggestion of circularity, with 'you' and 'all' being different points on the circle. This circularity is linked to the idea of eternal recurrence, that tragic sense of time that haunts the poem.

It is important to realise, however, that the initial movement from the particular 'you' to the universal 'all' is not direct. It reaches there by first passing through the 'you' of line 5, the only other time that this pronoun occurs in the poem's eleven lines. Now, in spite of the exclamation mark that punctuates the end of the line, suggesting an insistent directness, the 'you' of line 5 has taken on a more impersonal — or, more strictly, an 'indefinite personal' and generalised sense, like the French '*on*'. (This use as an indefinite personal pronoun is one of the special uses of the pronoun 'you' noted in the *Oxford English Dictionary* and is for denoting 'any hearer or reader: one, any one'.) And it acquires this impersonal and generalised meaning because the 'you' of line 5 is the culmination of a sequence: *speck-hero-monster-you*. This sense of the 'you' as more impersonal and generalised than personal and particular, is reinforced by the switch from the 'you' of line 5 to the 'all' of lines 10 and 11. A definite distance separates the 'you' of the title from the 'you' of line 5.

As we shall see later, the 'you' of the title and the 'you' of line 5, as subjects in both the grammatical and philosophical senses, also govern two different verbs and processes: 'are involved' and 'are consumed'.

'Consumed' is obviously not simply the re-statement or repetition of the idea informing 'involved'. It is an advance on it.

What we find is that the distance that separates the 'you' of the title from the 'you' of line 5 is matched by that which separates 'involved' from 'consumed':

>   you are involved
>   +   +
>   you are consumed

The narrator (the 'I' of line 1) is caught up in a similar movement as the reader/s: *I-you-all-all*. It is the same movement from the particular *I* to the universal *all*. (But we will return to the narrator later.) It is important to our argument that these movements which we are describing be understood as taking place *within* the experience of the poem: they constitute part of its process, its coming into being. And, most importantly, it is a process which is activated by the presence of the reader and by the act of reading.

Our little poem belongs in the company of those works of art, like impressionist paintings, which exist *in statu nascendi* (in a state of being born).[5] They are not closed and finished things, but require the activity of the reader or spectator to bring them to life and completion, to finish them. From the very first word of the title, the reader is implicated, not only in the dark time of the world, but also in the labour of the poem itself.

There are five verbs or verb structures in the poem.

Two are repeated: 'are involved' and 'are consumed'. All are rooted in the present. Even 'have learnt' is in the perfect tense. Not 'I learned,' which would have been preterite. Whereas the preterite would have cut the links between the present and the past, the perfect anchors the past into the present. This sense of the present contributes

---

5. This useful distinction is made by Ortega in his quirky but symptomatic 1925 essay, 'Notes on the Novel': 'A novelist must proceed in the same way as the impressionistic painters who set down on canvas such elements as the spectator needs for seeing an apple, and leave it to him to give to this material the finishing touches. Hence the fresh taste of all impressionistic painting. We seem to see the objects of the picture in a perpetual *status nascendi*'. He contrasts this to the 'finished' and 'mummified' presentation of the objects of non-impressionistic, i.e. representational painting. Jose Ortega y Gasset, *The Dehumanisation of Art & Notes on The Novel* (Princeton University Press, Princeton, NJ, 1972, p.64.

to the urgency pulsing through the poem. I will return to this idea later.

Of the five verb structures, four involve the past participle.

Contrast this with 'Proem,' that other poem of process, where there is an overwhelming frequency of the present participle (*saying, questioning, being, living*, etc.).

What is the effect of this preponderance of past participles in the poem: *involved, learnt, consumed, spun*? They suggest that we are in the realm of the done, even the done for. The accumulated sense is one of fatality, doom and powerlessness to affect the state of things. Which is why the poem is not one of militancy and exhortation, but of anguish and a certain stoic calm.

But the more important effect of the past participles is to set up, within the poem's logic of meaning, an opposition between the stasis of the done, in the domain of the object, and the movement we have described above, in the domain of the subject. This opposition is an important source of the poem's tension. That is, it is another motion within the poem.

And within the world of the past participles that is static in relation to the mobility of the pronouns, there is the movement — from 'involved' to 'consumed' — that is the poem's key movement, the source of its deepest drama.

Note that, in a poem of so few words, 'involved' and 'consumed' each occurs twice, and in the most strategic of places, at the beginning and at the end. They mark the beginning (involved) and end (consumed) of the first stanza and constitute the final crescendo of the second: they announce the opening and closing of the poem's two movements in the musical sense.

What of the verb not containing the past participle?

There is only one: 'shakes' in line 8. Working actively, transitively and intransitively, it occurs in the first of the poem's two similes:

> Like a jig
> shakes the loom.
> Like a web
> is spun the pattern

The similes constitute the body of the second stanza. The one follows the other in immediate succession; they resemble each other and seem to be symmetrical. They are in fact different and enter, through their very differences, into complex relations with each other:

1. jig : loom
2. web : pattern

Clearly, 'web' is to 'pattern' differently from 'jig' is to 'loom'. A web *is* a pattern; it is like it in itself, it is spun like it. The relation of 'jig' to 'loom,' on the other hand, is wholly dependent on the operations of the verb 'shakes'. There is no relation of likeness other than those established by the verb 'shakes'. And how does 'shakes' operate? It operates *actively*, transitively and intransitively.

It is transitive when it is the action of the subject 'jig' in an unabridged clause: 'A jig/shakes the loom.'

'Jig' is a word of uncertain origin and is used to mean two different things in the poem:

(i) a mechanical contrivance that activates another machine, like a loom;

(ii) a dance.

When 'shakes' is intransitive, it is governed by the subject 'loom' following its verb: 'shakes the loom,' or, prosaically, 'the loom shakes'. 'Shakes' establishes the likeness which is of the movement of the loom to a jig. In this intransitive operation of 'shakes,' 'jig' is being used in its second sense.

Depending on whether 'shakes' is working transitively or intransitively, important differences also arise in the use of the relational 'like' within simile 1. When 'shakes' is transitive, 'like' works as a conjunction to introduce the unabridged clause: 'a jig/shakes the loom.' When, on the other hand, 'shakes' is intransitive, 'like' works as a preposition to govern a noun: 'a jig'.

As the only verb of *activity* within the body of the narrator's story (that is, from line 2 to line 11) 'shakes' is in striking contrast to the verbs containing the past participle, which express an accomplished state. Whether in its transitive or its intransitive function, 'shakes' is the only verb in the poem which expresses the principle of *activity*.

In simile 2, 'like' also enjoys a dual function, that is, it works here also both as a preposition governing a noun ('like a web') and as a conjunction introducing an unabridged clause. But in simile 2, this conjunctional use is concealed, or retracted. This is so because the verb of the unabridged clause is suppressed:

> Like a web [is spun]
> is spun the pattern

The retraction of one of the two functions of 'like' brings about a contraction of the simile as a whole. It is now a simile in transition to a metaphor. An encyclopaedia of poetics states the difference:

> Whereas metaphor is a mode of condensation and compression, simile through its descriptive function readily leads to diffuseness and extension, even to the digressive development of the figurative scene, action or object as an object of beauty.

This compression of simile 2, especially after the very extended behaviour of its predecessor, is expressive of the movement that has been demonstrated in the poem's other verbal arrangements.

So, from simile 1 to simile 2, the ground has shifted: one of the two grammatical functions of 'like' is retracted, the objects of the comparison are alike in and of themselves and result from the same activity — spinning. And most importantly, we have passed from the realm of the active ('shakes') into the realm of the passive ('is spun'). This movement from activity to passivity is one of the two motions within the second stanza.

But the two similes do not express simply a movement from one state to another, or two distinct and separate stages of a single process. A rare punctuation mark, the poem's only full stop, is there to keep them apart. Yet they are joined. For even when confined in its transitive function by the subject 'jig' and the object 'loom', the verb 'shakes' exerts its 'intransitive' influence, that results from its subject's activity: the spinning of the loom, on to the *web* and *pattern* of simile 2. It reaches into the second simile and invites us to think of a web set trembling by the slightest movement on any single one of its strands.

The web that is spun and the loom that shakes like a jig are confirmed in their connection when we note that 'loom' and 'web' were once synonymous poetic usages, now obsolete. As in H. More in 1647:

> Like spider in her web, so do we sit
> Within this spirit and if ought do shake
> This subtile loom we feel as it doth hit

So the 'loom' of line 8 is both the instrument for weaving together separate strands and is itself webbed, or stringed. Even while one simile follows the other in immediate succession, a standard enough technique for multiplying likenesses, the second moves in the direction of passivity and prepares us for the movement within the poem's two final lines, its central motion. But it does so without quite leaving behind the activity principle of the loom as the creator of patterns.

And what is this pattern that is spun?

The loom is the great Loom of Fate which binds all together, that strengthening and realisation of the whole which is simultaneously a losing and negation of each individual part. The pattern that it weaves is the cosmic tapestry which expresses the idea central to fatalism: man is at the mercy of the gods. As in blinded Gloucester's cry of anguish: 'As flies to wanton boys, are we to th' Gods: They kill us for their sport'.

Such is our 'web' of line 9. The effect of the similes, and of the motion between them, strengthens the view that this is a poem of despair, almost Greek in its austerity, its sense of eternal recurrence, and the hopelessness of its vision.

The exclamation marks, three in all, bring to a close stanzas not overly disturbed by punctuation, and are the graphic signals of the poem's apocalyptic direction. In the loom shaking like a jig there is a suggestion of arbitrariness, of artlessness and heartlessness, with things falling as they might. It is an infernal machine. And there is after all, at the heart of the design, an element of chance and wilfulness, an absurdity under the circumstances.

This haphazardness of things, or contingency, is expressed more openly in the rapidity with which a 'speck' may become a 'hero,' a 'hero' a 'monster,' although the day of the monster is not named but is beyond tomorrow. But the Great Web is democratic: there is and will be room for all.

Involved, consumed, you are involved, you are consumed, all are involved, all are consumed — the refrain tolls through the poem and is choric in its function.

The movement from 'involved' to 'consumed' is the first and the last of the poem's movements, that which was in the beginning and which is at the end. It dictated the motions of the 'You' and of the 'like.' It is the poem's central motion, that which governs all its other motions and into which all other motions are drawn and converge.

In the drama of consciousness and utterance that is the poem, 'involved' and 'consumed' signify the two stages of the process of knowing. The moment at which *and within which* we pass from one into the other is the moment of a truth and of the knowledge of truth. In the language of speculative philosophy, it is the point at which the 'for-itself' of consciousness encounters the 'in-itself' of the world and act out their courtship and their conflict.

This zone of transaction where subject and object meet is what George Whalley, borrowing from the vocabulary of physics and neurology, calls the 'interface.' The interface is the zone of truth and reality, where all values reside. 'To be "involved" at the interface is to be "real," to engage in reality,' says Whalley. And the task of the poet, whose involvement at the interface most resembles that of the mystic, is 'to reveal "what it is like" at the interface'.[6] The poet does this by engaging in an 'event of reality,' an experience of such potency and depth that it drives him to apply the means of escaping the pull of its abyss which, because he is a poet, are means that are available to him. It is his mode of affirmation.

To such an 'event of reality' Whalley offers the word *paradeigmatic*:

> This term has two implications:
>
> (a) the form or archetype of human experience is to be found in paradeigmatic experience and not in the experience of everyday man in the workaday world; and
>
> (b) that this order of experience is its own argument, carries its own proof within itself, is at once an event

---

6. George Whalley, *Poetic Process, An Essay in Poetics*, (Meridian, NY, 1967, p.31.
'Let us imagine that man and nature (or 'subject' and 'object') meet and embrace each other at an interface, the interface being a pliable and permeable membrane extending infinitely both upwards and on either hand. This membrane is to be regarded as a medium *joining*, not separating, subject and object ... In actual life, subject and object interpenetrate each other; but since for purposeful action we must pretend that subject and object can be separated, the interface also represents this assumed separation'.

> of value and knowing... paradeigmatic experience is the responsive feeling of naked collision with reality: an intimate penetration into, or immersion in, reality.[7]

The poem is what springs from the experience of a paradeigmatic event. And the space between the event and the finished poem is where the activity of poetry takes place, where the poem is born and shaped.

For Whalley, this is the saving contract, the act and art of 'symbolic extrication':

> Symbolic extrication is the activity by which the poet extricates himself from an intolerable reality (the paradeigmatic event) by transferring his feeling for that reality to a system of symbols. The poem is not merely a by-product of that withdrawing movement but the necessary condition of it.[8]

In reproducing the passage from involvement to consumption, the poem does so in a way that suggests that the passage is ineluctable and somehow perilous. It has to be gotten over and gotten over with. This, I believe, is the source of the urgency which pulses in the poem. Expressing itself through particular organisations of language, this urgency has what can be called a psychological basis in the poem. In the re-enactment of the drama of consciousness that is the poem, it is the urgency driving the narrator to draw the conclusions out of his experience before it is too late: 'This I have learnt'.

By making 'this' the first word of the poem proper, a dislocation of the normal word order, the emphasis falls immediately on the lesson itself — he plunges us without ceremony in *medias res*. The 'I' is then jettisoned. It does not

---

7. *Ibid.*, p.31.
8. *Ibid.*, p.31.

reappear in the rest of the poem. In the sense suggested by the poem, it *dissolves* away. The narrator is enacting the urgency of the poet to rid himself of the terror of the paradeigmatic event. The experience of the event that is the origin of the poem occurs in the space just prior to the dissolution of the subject into the object. It is the subject's last act. It is the space of perception, the space of a final transaction between the subject and the object before the subject is devoured ('consumed') by the object. This consumption by the object is a consummation for the subject, something for which it yearns. ('Consume', in another obsolete usage, was once synonymous with 'consummate'.) This compulsion of the subject to be one with the object, in all its loathsomeness and fascination, is a shudder that runs through the poems of Martin Carter and is the subject matter itself of certain poems. It is the compulsion that sets the imagination in motion and provides the site of its unique drama: the subject/self poised, defiant and sentient, on the brink of its engulfment by and into the object/world, mute and mineral.

'To make a work of art,' writes Whalley, 'is for the artist an urgent and clamorous need: it is his only means of withdrawing from reality, and the work of art faithfully – ruthlessly – made is the only condition of his returning into contact with reality again.'[9]

When we speak of the poem being one of process, and call it dialectical, it is because it is made up of a webbed system of language, a complex of active and mobile language elements in dynamic interplay. Such a poem will yield a sense of itself as poem and tend to present or lay bare the play of its artifice and its stratagems. Even while conveying the most sombre of visions, it will speak for the interconnectedness of all things. The motions within such a poem will express and derive from the motion of all things.

---

9. *Ibid.*, p.105.

Nothing is separate from anything else, there is no identity without relationship, we are implicated in every relation to the real world of our fellow human beings and of nature, and we are condemned to the surroundings made for us by our history. And when we speak of the poem being one of truth, and call it art, it is because it is the necessary and shaped utterance of an experience of reality so potent and terrible that it is relieved only by its expression through and in the poem itself. Such a poem is born out of the death-wish of the subject.

'You are involved' is, in the last instance, a philosophical and religious poem that enacts the drama of its own creation — at once its genesis and its revelation. Coleridge says somewhere: 'to read Dryden and Pope, etc, you need only count syllables; but to read Donne you must measure *time*, and discover the time of each word by the sense of passion'. It is this sense of passion charging each word that burns so brightly in the slightest song of Blake and accounts for its radiance and its lyrical power.

It is not to be precious that we invoke the names of Donne and Blake and Coleridge. Nor is it merely because these visionaries of reality, with Dante and Yeats, are among the most revered of Martin Carter's poets. 'You are involved' comes to us out of an experience of reality that is essentially religious in the intensity of its conviction, in the humility of its frail humanity and in the spirituality of its concerns.

In the concluding arguments of his study of the advertisement, Spitzer shows how the 'for you' that ends its text is the re- emergence, in secular and laicised form, of a phrase:

> ...which can perhaps be traced back directly to statements of dogma made from the pulpit... When the pastor declares that 'Christ has suffered death for you, for the liberation of your soul from sin,' he is presenting this divine intervention as working for

each individual separately and his 'you' is interpreted by each of his listeners as a 'for me personally'.[10]

To call the poem philosophical and religious is also to say that it has a powerful ethical dimension. The narrator is, in fact, expressly created in his pitiful shivering humanity and speaks to and for us all out of human fellowship and human suffering. He stands for man in his human sensuousness who saves himself in that only human way, through the *logos* that was in the beginning and always is, through the altogether human and social act of language.

The narrator of 'You are involved' is sensuous suffering man crouched, like Blake's Newton, over the object of his original suffering. He is man in the 'abomination of desolation'.[11]

---

10. Spitzer, p.274.
11. In the words of Jesus:
> But when ye shall see the abomination of desolation, spoken of by Daniel the prophet, standing where it ought not, (let him that readeth understand,) then let them that be in Judea flee to the mountains.
> MARK 13:14; MATTHEW 24; 15-16.

For Blake, the 'abomination of desolation' resides in man's reasoning power, his capacity for abstraction which can become hostile to humanity when substituted for reality:

> And this is the manner of the Sons of Albion in their strength: they take the Two Contraries which are call'd Qualities, with which every Substance is clothed: they name them Good & Evil; from them they make an Abstract, which is a Negation not only of the substance from which it is derived, a murderer of its own Body, but also a murderer of every Divine Member: it is the Reasoning Power, an Abstract objecting power that Negatives every thing. This is the Spectre of Man, the Holy Reasoning Power, and in its Holiness is closed the Abomination of Desolation. (*Jerusalem* 10:7)

To these abstractions, Blake 'opposed the Visions of Imagination' (*Jerusalem* 74:26).

In 'You are involved' the landscape is empty. Nature is nowhere to be seen or felt. Unusually in 11 lines of Martin Carter there is not a tree nor a stone nor a sky to be seen.

He is fixed in no place, this 'I'. And because he occupies no particular place and can be anywhere, we are free to imagine him everywhere, within and without: he is archetypal.

'Man is an objective sensuous being, and because he feels what he suffers,' Marx writes in the *1844 Manuscripts*, 'a passionate being. Passion is the essential force of man energetically bent on its object'. And language, through which we are saved, Marx says of it: 'the element of thought itself, — the element of thought's living expression: language, is of a sensuous nature'.[12]

To return briefly to the verb '**shakes**', we can say that, in its transitive use, it is the only instance in the poem of something acting on something else: it is the action performed by the jig on the loom.

As such it raises up the problem of causes and of the first cause: who moves the jig that shakes the loom?

The absence of an originating agency, like a human hand, suggests the inhuman and so joins in the sense of fatalism that the dancing loom suggests when 'shakes' is intransitive. But this mysterious activation of the loom also opens up the empty space of human agency, and activates the ethical dimension of the poem. It is the place within the poem where we can enter the domain of the ethical, the domain of human action.

The ethical argument of the poem may go as follows: we are condemned to be involved because we are the active creatures of nature and of history and we can ignore or

---

12. Karl Marx, *The Economic & Philosophic Manuscripts of 1844* (International Publishers, NY, 1976) p. 182.

repudiate but not alter or undo the fact of that condemnation to involvement. Our every act is an intervention into the world of other human beings and alters (shakes), however minutely, the disposition of forces (web/pattern) that exist in the real world.

Human activity is transforming activity. At least one ethics of political commitment says that because this is so, human actions must be responsible and conscious actions and are most humanly directed when enlisted in the service of human freedom against forms of oppression and human suffering.

Human activity is transforming activity not because we choose it to be so: it is its lot. Actions based in such an understanding of ethics may — the fatalism of the poem suggests that it does and always will — lead to disastrous interventions which may be as private as the broken promise of a lover or as public as a political catastrophe. These failures, for our consolation and recuperation, we interpret or transform into instances of the eternal human condition, points on the wheel of history: in the moment of the most felt failure, time loses its linear way and turns into a circle. Repeated failure can tempt us, in self-defence, to turn fearful of intervention itself, except in the most mediated of ways, through acts of the mind which — if you are also a poet — may in the end be the truest and purest acts of all and the only true acts available.

This, if you like, is the ethics of the poem.

And it is an ethics of stoicism.

But we would do well to go beyond this, into the poem's deepest zones. We do this by following the poem where it leads. And it leads us by its words. Attempts to confine the poem to a statement about, or even to an experience of, an event of politics in the narrow sense, deprive it, or what is more our loss, make it deprive us of what are its most pressing dimensions and its own expressed urgencies: we narrow its range and limit its power. And it closes itself to us.

What we prefer to say, in this regard, is that in an environment of militancy and passion and discovery, in the bleak days when reaction and unreason held dominion over reason and revolution, or when the revolution lost dominion over itself and fell into unreason, a young poet brooded deeply and creatively about the large eternal things: truth, being, the one and the many, knowing and doing, birth, life and death.

At the heart of the brooding, whether sparked by the stem of a broken flower or by the turret of a gunboat, in its deepest depths, were sadness and dejection, a sharing in the lost hopes of a hopeful time.

In a season that promised birth, the generation of 1953 lived through the anguish and bitterness of the stillborn: This we have learnt.

To return now to the question with which we began these observations: why does this particular poem end *Poems of Resistance*?

I believe it is because it puts a certain stamp of completeness on and crowns and transfigures the *experience of the making of the previous poems*, many of which also have their dark and private spaces. Because, too, it is a poem of rupture and transition, an end and a beginning.

The dense, self-absorbed poems of Martin Carter's recent years are the destination, or better; a stage in the way (since the poet is still growing) of a poetic and philosophical journey that began at the beginning, in those militant and apparently least private poems of those so public days. And that which is encoded deep inside the early poems is to emerge more and more boldly, more and more insistently, in the later poems. Set down with such suppleness and lyrical confidence a quarter of a century later, 'Proem' is a meta-poem, speaking to us of its own becoming: the 'you' of 'Proem' is the poem itself.

The young poet-militant, from within the frontline of the people's freedom struggle, placed this spare and elegiac little luminous poem at the end of *Poems of Resistance* because, being a poet of truth and scruple, he could not but qualify the hope and temper the optimism of the battle songs. All was not light. And of all the sensitive fighters around him, it was he who looked most intently into the nightmare of our history and, in occasional flashes of darkness, he made his report of what he saw there. And in the nightmare of the present he has gone on reporting. It is why his friend Wilson Harris can say of him: 'Beneath the flamboyance, flag or shirt for the revolution, lies mingled horror and hope'.[13] And it was precisely in the moments of most intense darkness that he reflected most intensely on the act of poetry itself and registered its passion and its glory.

From the outset a poet true to his calling, Martin Carter has never been deaf to the siren-song of poetry itself, whispering above the clamour, as it has whispered down through the ages, that 'its political mission is to refuse any political mission and to continue to speak for everyone about things of which no one speaks, of a tree, a stone, of that which does not exist'.[14]

The siren still sings in his ear.

Today, in a bleak time, her song comes piercing the wind. It is pure and clear.[15]

---

13. *Explorations*, p. 8.
14. Hans Magnus Enzensberger, 'Poetry and Politics,' in *The Consciousness Industry, On Literature, Politics and the Media* (Seabury, NY 1974), p. 81.
15. The question that now arises is why does this little poem disappear. It is absent from the selection from *Poems of Resistance* which reappears in *Poems of Succession*, forming one of its parts in the architecture of the whole. The answer belongs to the story of *Poems of Succession* which is yet to be told. Suffice it to say, for now, that 'Proem' holds the key.

...my Abstract folly hurries me often away. While I am at work, carrying me over Mountains & Valleys, which are not Real, in a Land of Abstraction where Spectres of the Dead wander.

— **William Blake**

The Poems of October which follow were written in the spaces of the essay on 'You are Involved'. That is to say, they are of one weave. For it is so that I have thought them, the essay and the poems together and within.

— RR

REQUIEM FOR LOUIS LA ROCHE
30 September 1913 — 13 October 1986)

Louis La Roche, my friend,
A straight-backed, three-legged chair,
Carved intricately turned and fretted
Over a hundred years old
Will remind me of your
Hands
Which would have shaped
The fourth and curling thing
To make the other three stand and stare
At their ancient exquisite fellow
Come spryly back again.

Louis LaRoche, my friend,
A lovely painting inside an ugly frame,
Shafts of colour glancing off lovely skin
Under a hundred years old
Will remind me of your
Hands
Which would have brushed
A frame of glory
To tempt the varnished beauty
To step out of the picture
Leaving your frame alone
To glow
Around an empty space.

Louis LaRoche, my friend,
A guitar against an empty wall,
Curved and lush and taut
Will remind me of your

Hands
Which made music of the wood
From which music has fled
Leaving silence alone
To pay tribute to sound.

Louis LaRoche, my friend,
Maître of 73 human years,
Master carver
Unbowed image-maker
Musician
Gentle friend, Louis LaRoche,
I think now of the legion of perfect shapes
That hallow the rooms
Even of the unworthy,
Shining things and true
Of wood
That honour the great trees
At the hour of their death
Because they are their finest selves
In your final forms.

YOUR OCTOBER WORDS
(for B)

Words can be cold and hard
Like ice
That reminds even the sun
Of the limits
Of its fire
In zones where ice is
Mistress
Over earth and sky.

Words can be warm and soft
Like throat
Of little bird
Whose broken wing
Saddens even the air
Which is less even than itself
Without the fluttering
Of this particular wing.

Words can be hot and holy
Like sacred fire
That licks at the lips
Of the simple dish
As the lies of the world
Are burned away
In flames of truth
Off a martyr's pyre.

The words you have brought me
This night in October
Are like all of these things
As I think of you
With my words.

JUNE AND OCTOBER
(for my son and all the children)

The poem is sparked
By the stem of a broken flower
Or by the turret of a gunboat
In the harbour.

★

You were in yourselves different
From other friends
Although each friend is different
From every other.
You were less different
From each other
In the end
Where you and death came face
to face
At the rendezvous of defeat
In absolute space.

What joins you in my mind
Across your differences
Is not only
That I tasted the smoke
Raw in the throat
Of both holy pyres
Blown to me
Across hill and valley
Through cross-hairs of streets
Of murderous city,

But that the two of you
In death
Loosened floods of grief
Which were nothing more
Than the banked streams
Of the love
Your lives watered
Alive
Bursting free.

Walter & Maurice
Rodney and Bishop
Maurice & Walter
June and October
The year's prime and its dying,
Your names tangle in my mind
As across the years
I weave you these my words
While sorrow holds me
In her arms.

IMAGES OF OCTOBER
(for Vanda)

The images of October
Are tinged with darkness.
They come still with the stillness
Of the hollows of an empty
cathedral
In the dead of night
When the faithful have departed.
And stillness only is
A gaze of love that is
His still undying sight.

The music of October
Is haunted with the sadness
That trembles on the air
When an old musician dies
And a young workingman
Blows a sweet melody
Through the chambers of his horn
Over the grave
At the hour of his entry
Into the cold heart
Of the land.

The dreams of October
Are lit with the light
That glows
From the deeds
That flower
From the seeds of human love

Planted true and deep
Atoms of fire
Into the cold heart
Of the land.

The words of October
Are full
Of all the things
Of which words are
Always full.
They come trailing the pure agony
Of their ancient nativity
At journey's end,
Worn and weary things
That have journeyed far
Across the years
Up through the seas
From the cleaner beds
Of my deepest self.

Is it any wonder
That I should sorrow
In the month of October
And speak of it
In words I remember
As fusing together lost limbs
Is the remembering
Of the body
That once was one?

LIGHT STEPS IN OCTOBER: A SERENADE
(for C)

One midsummer night
You danced and warbled
Prettily
Into the ear of my mind
Which hears you now
At an unlikely time
In October
Warbling prettily
In the ear
Of my mind.

The words you sent
From a room warm
In the cold
Reached me in October
And sparked
October thoughts
Which in their truth
Must say
That you warbled
Your midsummer way
Into my October mind.

Must mind probe mind
And lend his ear
To the words that fluttered
In the air
Of the time

That you warbled
Prettily
Into the ear
of my mind?

Not at all.
Let mind instead
Explain to mind
In words that are clear
Why mind should hear
Your warbles at all
In the month of October
In the sad midst
of the still things
Of the fall.

After all,
We exchanged few words
That night in midsummer
And even shared some words
As I do recall.
Truth to tell, It was not the words
At all.
They were light
Fluttering things
Quick and bright
Well mannered
Well travelled
Words of the shortest life,
Living as fireflies live
In the darkness
Of which they only are
The only lies.

Was it nothing
More or less
Than that the grip of a soft
Hand on a wrist
One midsummer night
Was longer
And stronger
Than wrist is to be gripped
By a dark and sprightly sister
Alive with the light
Of mischievous moon
High
In midsummer sky?

Mind must counsel mind.
Words can say
All in all
To mind,
But words are no match
For long held wrist
By dark and sprightly sister
Silent with the sound
Of whispering spring
Deep
In midsummer ground.

In the face
Of the touch of love
Words are feeble things
Most of use
In naming the loss
That the touch
Left upon a face.

But see how prettily
You have warbled your way
Among my October words
Tripping light and daintily
Across the beds of pain
In the gardens
Of sorrow,
Midsummer breeze
Through leafless trees
In freezing wintertime.

OCTOBER PLEASANTRY
(for M on listening to Robyn Archer sing the songs of Brecht)

It occurs to me
As I rest from serious work
That in the alphabetical arrangement
Of the books on my shelf
No poet stands between
My Carter and my Brecht.

It is of some interest though
That Blake comes before
Donne with Dante after.
At the very end
Stand Yeats and Virgil,
The one taking refuge in visions
Mindful of actions
In the torment of the world,
The other lighting our way
To the darkest of places
In the regions that lie lowest
In the vast spaces
Of the soul,
Even in lines that he wrote
An emperor to promote.

No poet stands between
My Carter and my Brecht,
The one who thinks justly
In music of freedom

That will cleanse the world
Of its habits of sin,
The other who sings of a world
Free of disaster
Where every little servant
Knows he's master.

In the alphabetical arrangement
Of the books on my shelf
No poet stands between
My Carter and my Brecht.

OF MUSIC IN OCTOBER
(for Leila, little sister of the violin)

It is quite out of the ordinary
How these my songs of October
Sing themselves
Through and out
Of my mind.

Words alone
Do not suffice
To tell of what happens
In the spaces
Around and above
And below,
After and before
The words themselves.

Curiously, it is
In this emptiness
Of silent space
That words live
Most of their sleeping lives,
Possessions of others
Which only awake
To become
Possessions for me
When each comes
Out of the dark,
Alone or in company
Of comfortable friends
Who may be old or new

And work their way
Singly or together
In and around
After and below
Above and before
The words of others
Which have done
And come
Into my possession
Before the new arrivals
Reach
Journey's end
To sing all
Together
In these songs of October
That make all things
New again.

My words go
In their quandary
To a luminous man of words
That inscribed DIONYSOS
At the foot of the cross
Of the holy fire
Into whose blaze of truth
His words had led him
Out of his mind.

It is of noble Nietzsche
In torment
That I think
In these words
Of October
That now

In this instant itself
Become
Possessions for me
Alone and together
Singing themselves
Through and out
Of my mind.

It is to music
That he went
After the descent
Of words
Had ended
Out of words
He knew
As I know too
It is only music alone
That can say
In the ways
Of itself
All of which ways
Are at home
In space
Why words journey
Alone and together
Out of the spaces
Of the darkness
Of their sleeping lives,
Becoming
More and more awake
As they weary
More and more
To journey's end
And come to rest

On the bars of peace
Of purest sound
Awake at last
To the full glory
Of themselves.

WORDS OF SHAME

It comes to my mind
That among the words
And songs
Of my October
There are no songs
In words
For you.

How could this be
When all of my words
Of six Octobers
Dwelled in the places
You gave them
In the world
And in my mind
Wore colours and formed shapes
To please you best
Of all those
With whom I spent myself
In my words
Of six Octobers?

The October words
That come
Into my mind
Now that October
Nears its end
And final fall,
Say in their truth
Of October

That they come in shame
To your door
Before you
To confess
That they can sweeter sing
Away from you
And within,
For that of you
That is
Within me,
Not without.

TAKE THESE THE GIFT:
Poem For Eusi

Take these the gift
Of my October words
You from whose pen
Storm squadrons of words
Fierce and cunning
Exact in formation
Agile and righteous
As warriors in the veldt
On the hunt of the just
Spoils that will be
Loaves for the hungry
In the first feast of the world
To forever finish
With banquets of the rich
Wicked amid puffed lips
Of your hungry multitudes
Of your children
Wasting in the dust.

I mean all of these words
That have fallen
Like the rains of October
On the dry sands of my heart
As a silkworm
Means the silk
It must lose to live.

Vertical man of the open mind
Easy with grace,
As I send you these the gift

Of my October words
I think of him you have long loved
Before whose greatness of soul
Even the haughty Himalayas
Shrank into themselves
At holiness that walked
Barefoot in cotton cloth
Upon the Indian earth
In the thick of the simplest
To be found
Under the Indian sun.

I think of him now
As I sing
This my October song
When in words
That were stern and supple
Yet full of grace and serene
Wonder
He rebuked a great poet that he loved
For the shadow of the lovely bird
That he sang soaring in splendour
Across the Indian sky
Fell across the path
Of a hungry man
Who could not even walk the earth
Much less be glad
That even such a bird as this
Once did fly
Across the Indian sky.

Yet I have been made glad
That the words of October
Fell freely
Like the clean rains of October
On the dry dust
Of the land.

Take these the gift
Of my free October words
Of the heart
Of the land
For you.

ODE FOR SAMORA MACHEL
(to Bishop Randolph George)

If ever doubt there was
That October is
Month of earth's agony
And of its rebirth
Before and inside
The season of its death,
World's fall
Into the fall of the year,
An aeroplane falling
Out of the clear blue
Of an African sky,
Like a rock
That is the congealed sorrows
Of the ages
Rolled into one ball,
One single sphere
Of perfect pain
That is the world
Falling
Out of grace
Again,
Into the hour of the furnace
Of an African day,
Would have silenced
The word of doubt
That every believer knows
Is the sigh of truth
In a sinner's throat.

If ever doubt there was
That October is
Month of world's agony
And of its rebirth
Earth's fall
Into the fall of the year,
Word of your death
Brought on winds of October
Would have settled the matter
Now and hereafter,
Word of your death
That every sinner knows
Is the worm in the fruit
Of the tree of hate
In the orchard of love
From which he is chased
With words of scorn and fire
For the waste
That is born
In every nightblack sin
Of his lilywhite hand.

RETURN TO REASON, AN EKPHRASIS
(for Horace Taitt, Psychiatrist)

I

October words
For you,
My brother in mind,
Must unnaturally begin
Not in words
At all.

For what is there
In the ways of words
That I can tell
You of all others
Who spend your words
Cradling the words
Of others?

To cradle
The words of others
Is not first
To know
And then to love
The other
Through his words,
Nor first
To love
And then to know
The other
Through his words.

No, my brother in mind,
October words
For you
Must unnaturally begin
Not in words
At all.

II

So I choose to begin
My October song
For you
In an image
From a book
That is of images
And words
(Of which
Some are true
October words.)
It is an image
That drifts
From the light
To the dark
And back to light
Again,
Of lines that are
Thick and thin
But never straight.
There is even a point
At which white
And black
Make contact:
A cord of grey
Hangs white

From black
At a lovely angle,
Joining black to white
In space triangular
Of lines that are thin
Meeting hypotenuse
That is thick
And marred
By spot or patch
More or less
At its centre.
All lines are grey,
The spot or patch
Is black.
It is path, perhaps,
That runs from bank of one side
That is white
To bank of the other
That is black.
This cord,
Or path, whatever,
Runs over and through
Spot or patch
That is
Navel of woman,
Soft centre
Of starting world.
Or, if you prefer,
(Which I doubt)
Only the frayed strands
Of the cord
Or a murky puddle
In the path.

Man Ray

The Return to Reason (Retour á la Raison)

1923 18.7 x 13.9 cm.

Julian Levy Collection, Special Photography Acquisitions

COURTESY OF THE ART INSTITUTE OF CHICAGO

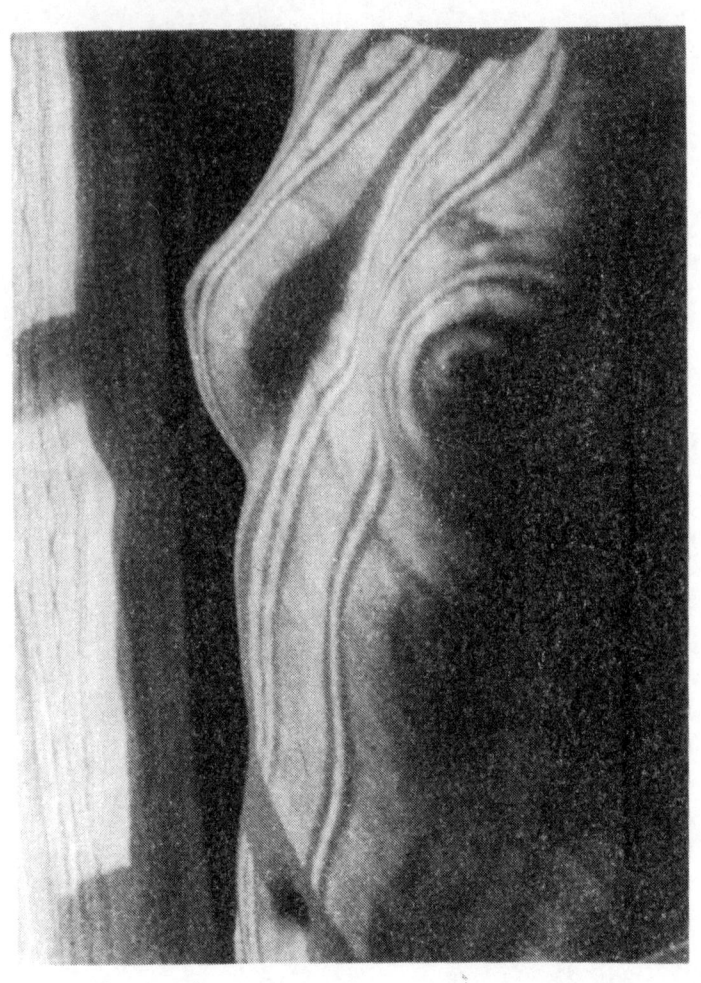

She is standing
At a window
Half in shade
And half in light
Half of her in all,
Chest and breasts
And belly revealed,
Lacerated by the light
Flowing through the web
Of a lace curtain
In a room
Somewhere.

Her right breast
Faces the sun,
Her left breast
Faces me.
The patterns the sun
Brands
On her sun
Turned body
Are soft streams
Of white
That curl and flow
From neck to navel
And below,
Coursing over and round
Breast for sun
And breast for me
That is still pond
Circled
With ripples of light
Around the dark.

The origin
Of this image
Hangs
In the Julien Levy Collection
In the Art
Institute of Chicago.
It was made
In 1923 in Paris
By a man
With a camera
Named Man Ray.

Its name in words
Is
Retour à la Raison,
Return to Reason.

III

I dare tarry no longer
Among these words
Of October
That have led me
To self's still centre
Where nothing is
Near the end
Of the final fall
At the start
Of words
And of all
Of world
This world that is
Still
Beyond the edge

Is amazingly
And horribly
A cold space and pure
Of the most perfect forms.

So fare me well,
Brother in mind,
And cradle you
These my words
Of the October
Of my mind
To know me
In the love
That you see
Of the me
To love in these
My October words
That you
Of all others
Know
Came freely singing
Through the dark well
Of being
Off the cleaner beds
Of my final self.
You of mind can see
They are in the beginning
And in the end,
Not unnaturally
Words of October
For me.

SONG AT POINT OF PATH
(for Vladimir Mayakovsky)

I will tarry no longer
In this web
Of October.
The world of human action
Is safer and better
By far.

A strand of cord
Of fraying strands
Joining white to black
Is thread of woman
Ariadne brings
For the stranded
In the maze
To come back
From hole of the beast
In well of the cave
Of pit of the soul.

A path that runs
From bank to bank
Joining black to white
Is path of world
On which hungry man
Sets weary foot
And glorious bird
Throws dark shadow
Of wing of death
Across the land
In bed of pain.

At point of cord
And point of path
To world of human action
I hear in the air
Of my mind
Clear throat of singer
Of mind
That is to man
And to woman
In labour of the world
At its making
Song of hope and glory
In human action
That is safer and better
By far.

As I draw closer
To journey's end
In world of human action
I see his poet's brow
Above his poet's mane
With the navel
In the head
The bullet tore
To shatter the mind
Of perfect forms.

Poet sublime
Of a better October
Of swollen rage
Of revolting man
When titans arose
Out of the slaughter
Of the innocents

In the shallow trenches
Of the world
To drive tsars and emperors
And their bankers too
Out of mind
With fury of fire
To cleanse the world
Of its habits of sin.

Vladimir Vladimirovich,
It is you that I hear.
At point of cord
And point of path
At journey's end
In world of human action
That is safer and better
By far.

But in truth
Of October
You come into these
My last October words
Not for your hymns of glory
In human action,
But for the absolute truth
Of the hole
In the temple
Of shining forms.

The world of human action
Is safer and better by far
For being world
Of imperfect forms
At home in imperfect world:

For poets of October
Who have dwelled
In the pure
And in the cold
Of still October space
It is safer and better
To have no revolver
In April or October.

Your last of words
You nailed on cross
Of sinful world
Are words of October
In April of the bullet
And I will forever
Cradle them
In the arms
Of my words:
'Stay happy'.

'Stay happy' is the last message in
Mayakovsky's suicide note of April
12, 1930, (RR)

IN MEMORIAM:
AUGUSTA JULIANA
MENDONCA READ
(11 March 1906 — 28 October
1986)

Augusta Juliana, girl
Of eyes
Slow to rise
And fall
And fingers
Quick to purl
And pick and twirl
Webs of silken dreams
Of forms
Blooming bright
In dying light
Of your last October days.

Augusta Juliana, girl,
As October died
You held to life
As if to keep faith
With unspoken promise
Not to become one
With stillness
Of October space.

I shall forever see
Your old October eyes
Searching out the boats
That did not drift

On indifferent sea
Across narrow window
Of your ebbing October world.

I shall forever hear
You tell in wonder
Of lovely cloud of gold
Wrapping you in its fold
As days grew short and cold
To make way
For night's long and final say.

That last time
We spoke together
You told in wonder
Of wondrous fellow
Who summoned you back
From night's domain
As son of mercy
With touch to conquer pain.

Augusta Juliana, girl,
I did not see you home
That last October day,
Boy astray and worthless
You rose to bless
With woman's healing kiss,
But good companions
Of journey's end
Say you turned and wept
As you rose and left
This imperfect place
Though in your ear
You heard in truth

Bell of grace
Tolling song of glory
In shining space.

Augusta Juliana, girl,
Quick of wit
And gentle tongue,
I did so wish
Deep in my October heart
That you of all others
Would have no part
In October sorrow.
But in the end
And final fall
In cloudless sky
At height of day
Fleece of gold
Of cloud's embrace.
Wrapped you tight
In precious fold
To carry you home
To hallowed space.

Augusta Juliana, girl,
I would have so preferred
Had there never been
Words of October sorrow
For you.

Augusta Juliana, girl,
I say simply
In the end
And final fall
That you fell

As the great trees fall
Leaving sky and earth
To wonder
At sudden space
Root and leaf
On leaving left
Emptier world to face.

*Georgetown,
October 13-31, 1986*

THE GREAT DARK (1973)

Orbiting, the sun itself has a sun
as the moon an earth, a man a mind.
And life is not a matter of a mother only.
It is also a question of the probability of the spirit,
strength of the web of the ever-weaving weaver
I know not how to speak of, caught as I am
in the great dark of the bright connection of words.

And the linked power of love holds the restless wind
even though the sky shudders, and life orbits
around time, around death, it holds the restless wind
as each might hold each other, as each might hold each other.

Martin Carter,
Poems of Succession

NOTES TO POEMS

p.29　Louis LaRoche, Master Carver and Violin Maker, died on October 13, 1986 after being hit by a car driven by the son of a Georgetown cinema owner.

p.29　'Which would have brushed', *brush* – a word in everyday use among carpenters and joiners in Guyana (and perhaps elsewhere) to signify the action of planing an already planed surface, the final and finishing passes of the plane over a surface.

p.50　Speaking of 'Ode on a Grecian Urn,' Spitzer asks: '*What is the whole poem about*, in the simplest, most obvious terms? It is first of all a description of an urn – that is, it belongs to the genre, known to Occidental literature from Homer and Theocritus to the Parnassians and Rilke, of the *ekphrasis*, the poetic description of a pictorial or sculptural work of art, which description implies, in the words of Théophile Gautier, 'une transposition d'art,' the reproduction, through the medium of words, of sensuously perceptible *objets d'arts* ('ut pictura poesis') Spitzer, p.72.

p.62　'She leaves us an example of endless industry, to borrow Wordsworth. Her imagination, her hands, her artistic taste were forever engaged in turning out, through the medium of crochet and embroidery, things of exciting beauty. A Guyanese poet I have the honour to call brother has watched her 'fingers quick to purl/ And pick and twirl/ Webs of Silken dreams...' (from the Eulogy by Eusi Kwayana for Augusta Read).

Rupert Roopnaraine was born in Kitty Village, Guyana in January 1943. One of the second batch of students to benefit from the introduction of free secondary education by the first PPP government, he entered Queen's College, Georgetown in 1953 as a County Scholar. In 1962, he entered St. John's College, Cambridge as a Guyana Scholar, where he studied Romance Languages. In 1970, he was awarded an HSS Fellowship to Cornell University where he completed his doctoral research with a dissertation on Dickens. He stayed on to teach in the Comparative Literature Department at Cornell until 1976 when he returned to Guyana. He has since then been Senior Lecturer in English at the University of Guyana. He is the author and director of two documentary films: *The Terror and the Time: notes on repressive violence in Guyana*; and *Maha Shiva Ratri, an experience in belief*.

A founder-member of the Working People's Alliance, he serves on the party's Central Committee and Political Bureau.